I0467870

Employment outlook: 2010–2020

Occupational employment projections to 2020

Overall employment is projected to increase about 14 percent during the 2010–2020 decade with more than half a million new jobs expected for each of four occupations—registered nurses, retail salespersons, home health aides, and personal care aides; occupations that typically need postsecondary education for entry are projected to grow faster than average, but occupations that typically need a high school diploma or less will continue to represent more than half of all jobs

From 2010 to 2020, the U.S. economy is projected to add 20.5 million new jobs as total employment grows from nearly 143.1 million to more than 163.5 million. This 14.3-percent growth reflects the assumption of a full-employment economy in 2020. Out of 749 detailed occupations, 657 are projected to grow, while 92 are projected to decline. The fastest growth is expected among healthcare, personal care, and community and social service occupations.

The Bureau of Labor Statistics (BLS) produces these long-term projections of occupational employment to supply those who seek or provide career guidance with information on how the labor market is changing. In addition, policymakers and educational authorities use BLS employment projections for long-term policy planning. Finally, BLS projections are used by states in preparing state and area projections.

Detailed descriptions of more than 500 occupations, including reasons they are projected to grow or decline, are included in the *Occupational Outlook Handbook*, a BLS career guidance publication.[1]

This article focuses on broad results of the projections and is designed for those seeking a comprehensive overview of the projections data. Those seeking career guidance information and information on specific occupations will likely find the *Handbook* more suitable.

The first section of this article describes the factors that provide context for generating the occupational projections, including projections and assumptions for growth in the population, labor force, and gross domestic product (GDP). The next section describes the methods used to produce the occupational projections, as well as the concepts and terminology that will be used throughout the rest of the article. The third section looks at projections for major occupational groups and describes trends across groups. The fourth section presents projections for select detailed occupations: those that are growing the fastest, adding the most new jobs, declining most rapidly, or losing the most jobs. The fifth section discusses the concept of replacement needs—that is, the job openings that arise when workers leave an occupation permanently rather than those that arise from occupational growth. Finally, the last section describes the projections within the context of the new BLS education and training classification system.

Overview of BLS projections

The occupational projections presented in this article are the last step in the employment projections process. The process begins with projecting the population and labor force. From there, changes in the aggregate economy—GDP and its components—are projected. Next, projections are derived for consumers' final demand of products and services from each industry. Then the interplay of goods and services among industries, including intermediate demand, is used to project output by industry. Once industry output is projected, industry employment is calculated by projecting productivity and hours. Finally, projected staffing patterns are developed to distribute the projected industry employment to occupations. The assumptions and results of projections for the population, labor force, GDP, and industry output and employment are covered in more detail in other articles in this issue of the *Monthly Labor Review*.

The demographics of the U.S. population will have a prime role in shaping the future of the workforce. Between 2010 and 2020, the civilian noninstitutional population ages 16 and older is projected to grow by 25.2 million, or about 1.0 percent per year. However, as the baby-boom generation ages, the population will also shift to older age groups, with those ages 55 and older projected to increase their share of the population from 31.4 percent to 36.6 percent through the projections period. Because older people are less likely to be part of the labor force, the labor force will increase by only 10.5 million, or 0.7 percent per year, over the same decade.[2] Demographic changes are important for determining not just the size of the workforce but also the demand for goods and services. Because older people are more likely to purchase certain types of goods and services, notably health care, their growing share of the population affects the projections for industries and occupations that provide those goods or services.[3]

The aggregate economy is expected to grow, with GDP growth averaging 3.0 percent annually from 2010 to 2020.[4] This growth is faster than the growth in the labor force because labor productivity, as measured by output per hour, is projected to grow by 2.0 percent annually. GDP is projected to grow somewhat faster than in recent history as the economy recovers from the effects of the December 2007–June 2009 recession. BLS projections focus on long-term trends and do not project business cycle fluctuations. However, because many economic variables were at lower than normal levels in 2010, many growth rates, like that for the GDP, are projected to be faster than historical trends. In addition, as industries and occupations that experienced large declines during the recession rebound, they may have higher growth rates relative to industries and occupations that were less affected by the recession.[5]

Another variable affected by the recession is the unemployment rate, which averaged 9.6 percent in 2010. Among the assumptions used in projecting the overall economy is that there will be a full-employment economy in 2020. The unemployment rate associated with a full-employment economy in 2020 is 5.2 percent. The increase in the labor force combined with this decrease in the unemployment rate together leads to the projected growth in employment.

Employment growth will not occur evenly across all industries and classes of employment. Nonagricultural wage and salary employment accounts for about 9 out of 10 jobs; within this group, service-providing industries are projected to grow by 1.5 percent per year during the 2010–2020 decade, while goods-producing industries are projected to grow by 1.0 percent per year.[6] Agricultural jobs are projected to decline by 0.6 percent per year, while jobs for nonagricultural self-employed and unpaid family workers are projected to grow by 0.8 percent per year.

How BLS derives occupational projections

As noted above, occupational projections are made by applying projected staffing patterns to industry employment projections in order to distribute industry employment to occupations. To derive projected-year (2020) staffing patterns, BLS economists use qualitative and quantitative analyses to project how base-year (2010) staffing patterns are likely to change. They examine historical staffing pattern data and conduct research on factors that may affect the utilization of occupations within given industries during the projection decade. Some examples of factors are:

- *Automation*: technology or machinery replaces workers by performing some of their tasks. This will lower the need for those workers as the technology is implemented.

- *Productivity-enhancing technology*: similar to automation but makes workers more efficient at the task, making it possible for workers to accomplish the same amount of work that previously required more workers. This will drive down the utilization of workers.

- *Domestic or offshore outsourcing*: companies contract with another firm to perform specific tasks instead of hiring their own workers. This will drive down use of those workers in the companies that outsource the work but may increase utilization in another industry if the work is being outsourced domestically.

- *Changes in product mix*: shifts in what an industry is producing to reflect, for example, increased demand for a specific product or service. This will increase demand for some workers while decreasing the utilization of others whose job duties are not essential to production of the new products.

- *Organizational or work restructuring*: any type of change in duties to produce the same output. This may increase the utilization of some workers and decrease the utilization of others.

For each industry, projected wage and salary employment is distributed to occupations on the basis of the projected staffing pattern. Occupational employment data for self-employed and unpaid family workers are projected separately. Total projected occupational employment is the sum of the projected employment for each wage and salary industry, the self-employed, and unpaid family workers.

Drivers of growth and decline

From an occupational point of view, there are two main factors that impact employment growth or decline: 1) the growth of industries that employ the occupation, and 2) changes in the way those industries use the occupation. Looking at the latter, if occupations A and B are both employed in one industry but the demand for occupation A is increasing because of one of the factors previously discussed, we would expect occupation A to grow faster than B. Without such a change to the staffing pattern, occupations A and B would both grow at the same rate as the industry in which they are employed. On the other hand, if occupation C is employed in a different industry that is growing faster, then occupation C will grow faster than either occupation A or B. Even when changes to occupational utilization are factored in, industry growth still has a major impact on occupational growth rates. Occupations concentrated in fast-growing industries such as health care tend to grow faster than occupations in slower growing or declining industries such as mining.

To illustrate the impact of industry growth, consider two occupations that are concentrated in different industries: 98 percent of shoe machine operators and tenders work in leather and allied product manufacturing, while 95 percent of subway and streetcar operators are in local government. These industries are behaving differently: leather and allied product manufacturing is projected to decline, while local government is projected to grow. Neither of these occupations is projected to be utilized differently within these industries, so their projected growth rates reflect the growth of the industries they are concentrated in: shoe machine operators and tenders are projected to decline by 53.4 percent between 2010 and 2020, while subway and streetcar operators are projected to grow by 9.8 percent.

To illustrate the impact of changes in occupational utilization, consider two occupations that are concentrated in the postal service industry: postal service mail carriers and postal service mail sorters, processors, and processing machine operators. These occupations have different growth rates because the way they are being used is changing, leading to a projected staffing pattern different from the current staffing pattern. Postal service mail sorters, processors, and processing machine operators are expected to represent a smaller portion of the industry in the future, as technological improvements to automated sorting and processing equipment will increase productivity and reduce the need for these workers. Meanwhile, postal service mail carriers are projected to increase their share of the industry because carriers will continue to be needed to deliver mail even as overall employment in the postal service industry declines. Postal service industry employment is projected to decline by 27.7 percent, but because of the expected changes in occupational utilization, jobs for postal service mail carriers are only projected to decline by 12.0 percent, while jobs for postal service mail sorters, processors, and processing machine operators are projected to decline by 48.5 percent.

Numeric versus percent change

There are two ways to measure occupational growth or decline: numeric change (projected-year employment minus base-year employment) and percent change (numeric change divided by base-year employment). Both of these measures of growth or decline are important for different reasons, and when viewed together, they give a more complete view of the projected changes to the occupation and the workforce.

Percent change is especially useful when comparing the outlook for different occupations. Looking at percent change controls for the occupation's size in the base year and focuses on how the occupation is changing. For example, general and operations managers are projected to add 81,600 new jobs while interpreters and translators are projected to add 24,600. However, the general and operations managers occupation is much larger. When looking at growth rates, we see that general and operations managers are projected to grow by only 4.6 percent while interpreters and translators are projected to grow by 42.2 percent. The percent change provides a clearer comparison between these occupations. Employment of interpreters and translators will grow rapidly as companies increasingly need these workers to assist in conducting multinational business. Meanwhile, the employment of general and operations managers is projected to grow more slowly than average as these managers oversee larger areas of operations, leaving lower level management to other managerial specialties.

While percent change is useful for comparing what is happening in different occupations, it does not by itself give an idea of how many jobs are being added. For example, employment of industrial-organizational psychologists is projected to grow by 34.9 percent, while

cashiers' jobs are only projected to grow by 7.4 percent. This gives the impression that industrial-organizational psychologists have a much better job outlook, but they are a relatively small occupation and are projected to add only 800 new jobs. Meanwhile, cashiers is a very large occupation and, despite relatively slow growth, is projected to add 250,200 new jobs. Numeric employment change shows that many jobs can be created even if an occupation is not growing fast and gives a better understanding of how growth of the economy will be distributed among occupations. Numeric employment change is also useful when combined with occupational replacement needs to give a more complete view of the extent of opportunities to enter an occupation. (Job openings created by replacement needs will be discussed later in this article.)

As these examples show, the size of an occupation and the occupation's growth rate are both important in determining the number of new jobs that will be created. This is further illustrated in chart 1. Brickmasons and blockmasons are expected to add about 36,000 new jobs, as are dishwashers. However, brickmasons and blockmasons are growing almost 6 times as fast as dishwashers,

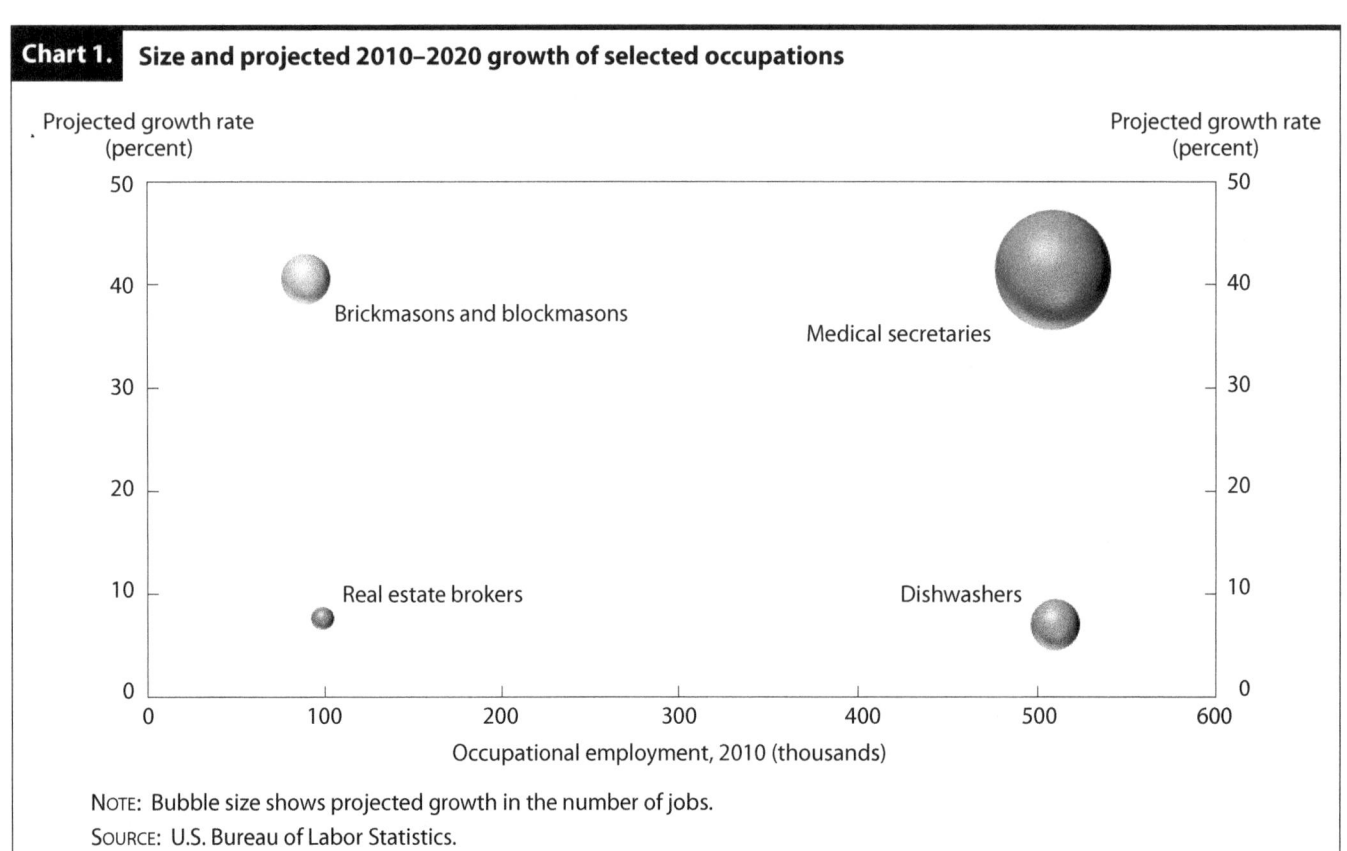

Chart 1. Size and projected 2010–2020 growth of selected occupations

NOTE: Bubble size shows projected growth in the number of jobs.
SOURCE: U.S. Bureau of Labor Statistics.

but because dishwashers make up a much larger occupation, the slower growth rate results in the same number of new jobs. If an occupation were growing at the same fast rate as brickmasons and blockmasons and were as large as dishwashers, it would add many more jobs; we see this with medical secretaries, an occupation which is expected to add 210,200 new jobs. In contrast, occupations that are both small and growing slowly, such as real estate brokers, add very few jobs. Visually, the closer an occupation is to the top right corner of chart 1, the larger its projected number of new jobs.

Occupational groups

To see some of the key changes affecting the economy over the projection period, it is easiest to examine the growth of the 22 major occupational groups. (See box on this page.) Changes in the employment levels of these groups also can serve to underline the effects of the recent recession on the projections. Table 1 presents the projections for the 22 major groups but also includes comparable data for 2006, a prerecession year.[7] Between 2006 and 2010, according to these data, the economy lost 7.6 million jobs, but the losses were not spread evenly across occupational groups. These recessionary employment declines can have a large impact on interpreting the projections through 2020. For example, the computer and mathematical occu-

pations group and the construction and extraction occupations group are projected to grow at similar rates, 22.0 percent and 22.2 percent, respectively. However, computer and mathematical occupations grew between 2006 and 2010, so their 2020 employment level will be 1.0 million higher than the level in 2006. On the other hand, construction and extraction employment fell rapidly after the burst of the housing bubble, so despite rapid growth from 2010 to 2020, the projected 2020 employment level is still below the 2006 level. (See chart 2.)

Like the projections for the construction and extraction group, projected employment levels for production occupations and transportation and material moving occupations are also below the levels of 2006, despite projected growth from 2010 to 2020. This is largely because the recession hit these three groups the hardest; they were the only groups where employment dropped by more than 10 percent from 2006 to 2010.

It also should be noted that rapid projected growth for some other occupational groups mostly represents recovering jobs lost between 2006 and 2010. Office and administrative support occupations is the group projected to add the most new jobs, 2.3 million, from 2010 to 2020. However, the group lost 1.7 million jobs from 2006 to 2010. Similarly, sales occupations are projected to add 1.9 million new jobs through 2020, but most of that is just the recovery of the 1.1 million jobs lost from 2006 to 2010.

How occupations are classified

BLS produces employment projections for 749 occupations; these occupations match the structure that the Occupational Employment Statistics (OES) program used to publish 2010 data, the primary source for base-year staffing patterns.[1] OES occupations are classified on the basis of the Standard Occupational Classification (SOC) system. However, OES data do not exactly match the updates made to the SOC in 2010. OES is transitioning to the 2010 SOC, but the change will not be fully implemented until the 2012 reference year.[2]

The coding structure has four levels of aggregation

(listed from most detailed to least): detailed occupations, broad occupations, minor groups, and major groups. Nearly all the 749 occupations are detailed occupations, and projections for all of these occupations are included on the Bureau of Labor Statistics website at **http://www.bls.gov/emp/ep_table_102.htm**. This article mostly discusses projections at the detailed occupation and major group level. However, the discussions of projections for particular major groups sometimes include references to the minor groups within that major group.

Notes

[1] Of the 749 occupations, 746 match OES directly. The remaining three—25–1000 postsecondary teachers, 29–1060 physicians and surgeons, and 45-2090 miscellaneous agricultural workers—are summary occupations that contain multiple

published OES occupations.

[2] For more information on differences between the 2010 SOC and the 2010 OES data, see **http://www.bls.gov/oes/oes_ques.htm#Ques41**.

Table 1. Employment and wages of major occupational groups, 2006, 2010, and projected 2020

(Numbers in thousands)

Matrix code	2010 National Employment Matrix title	Employment			Change, 2006–2010		Projected change, 2010–2020		Median annual wage, May 2010[1]
		2006	2010	2020	Number	Percent	Number	Percent	
00–0000	Total, all occupations	150,620.0	143,068.2	163,537.1	−7,551.8	−5.0	20,468.9	14.3	$33,840
11–0000	Management occupations	8,771.9	8,776.1	9,391.9	4.2	.0	615.8	7.0	91,440
13–0000	Business and financial operations occupations	6,831.9	6,789.2	7,961.7	−42.7	−.6	1,172.5	17.3	60,670
15–0000	Computer and mathematical occupations	3,313.2	3,542.8	4,321.1	229.6	6.9	778.3	22.0	73,720
17–0000	Architecture and engineering occupations	2,583.2	2,433.4	2,686.2	−149.8	−5.8	252.8	10.4	70,610
19–0000	Life, physical, and social science occupations	1,172.6	1,228.8	1,419.6	56.2	4.8	190.8	15.5	58,530
21–0000	Community and social service occupations	2,385.5	2,402.7	2,985.0	17.2	.7	582.3	24.2	39,280
23–0000	Legal occupations	1,222.2	1,211.9	1,342.9	−10.3	−.8	131.0	10.8	74,580
25–0000	Education, training, and library occupations	9,033.7	9,193.6	10,597.3	159.9	1.8	1,403.7	15.3	45,690
27–0000	Arts, design, entertainment, sports, and media occupations	2,677.0	2,708.5	3,051.0	31.5	1.2	342.5	12.6	42,870
29–0000	Healthcare practitioners and technical occupations	7,197.6	7,799.3	9,819.0	601.7	8.4	2,019.7	25.9	58,490
31–0000	Healthcare support occupations	3,723.5	4,190.0	5,633.7	466.5	12.5	1,443.7	34.5	24,760
33–0000	Protective service occupations	3,162.9	3,302.5	3,667.0	139.6	4.4	364.5	11.0	36,660
35–0000	Food preparation and serving related occupations	11,352.4	11,150.3	12,242.8	−202.1	−1.8	1,092.5	9.8	18,770
37–0000	Building and grounds cleaning and maintenance occupations	5,744.6	5,498.5	6,162.5	−246.1	−4.3	664.0	12.1	22,490
39–0000	Personal care and service occupations	4,877.6	4,994.7	6,331.4	117.1	2.4	1,336.6	26.8	20,640
41–0000	Sales and related occupations	15,985.4	14,915.6	16,784.7	−1,069.8	−6.7	1,869.1	12.5	24,370
43–0000	Office and administrative support occupations	24,344.0	22,602.5	24,938.2	−1,741.5	−7.2	2,335.7	10.3	30,710
45–0000	Farming, fishing, and forestry occupations	1,037.8	972.1	952.6	−65.7	−6.3	−19.4	−2.0	19,630
47–0000	Construction and extraction occupations	8,294.5	6,328.0	7,735.2	−1,966.5	−23.7	1,407.2	22.2	39,080
49–0000	Installation, maintenance, and repair occupations	5,883.3	5,428.6	6,228.7	−454.7	−7.7	800.2	14.7	40,120
51–0000	Production occupations	10,674.6	8,594.4	8,951.2	−2,080.2	−19.5	356.8	4.2	30,330
53–0000	Transportation and material moving occupations	10,350.8	9,004.8	10,333.4	−1,346.0	−13.0	1,328.7	14.8	28,400

[1] For wage and salary workers, from the Occupational Employment Statistics survey.

SOURCE: U.S. Bureau of Labor Statistics.

Chart 3 shows the employment trends for occupational groups whose employment declined by at least 2 percent from 2006 to 2010. Although growth is expected for all groups except farming, fishing, and forestry occupations (which is undergoing a long-term decline), none of these groups is expected to regain its employment share of 2006.

Chart 4 shows occupational groups that grew or de-clined by less than 2 percent from 2006 to 2010. These groups are all projected to grow, though with widely varying projected growth rates, from 2010 to 2020. Food preparation and serving occupations and management occupations are projected to grow slower than most of the occupations included on the chart, indicating that these two groups may not be strongly affected by business cy-

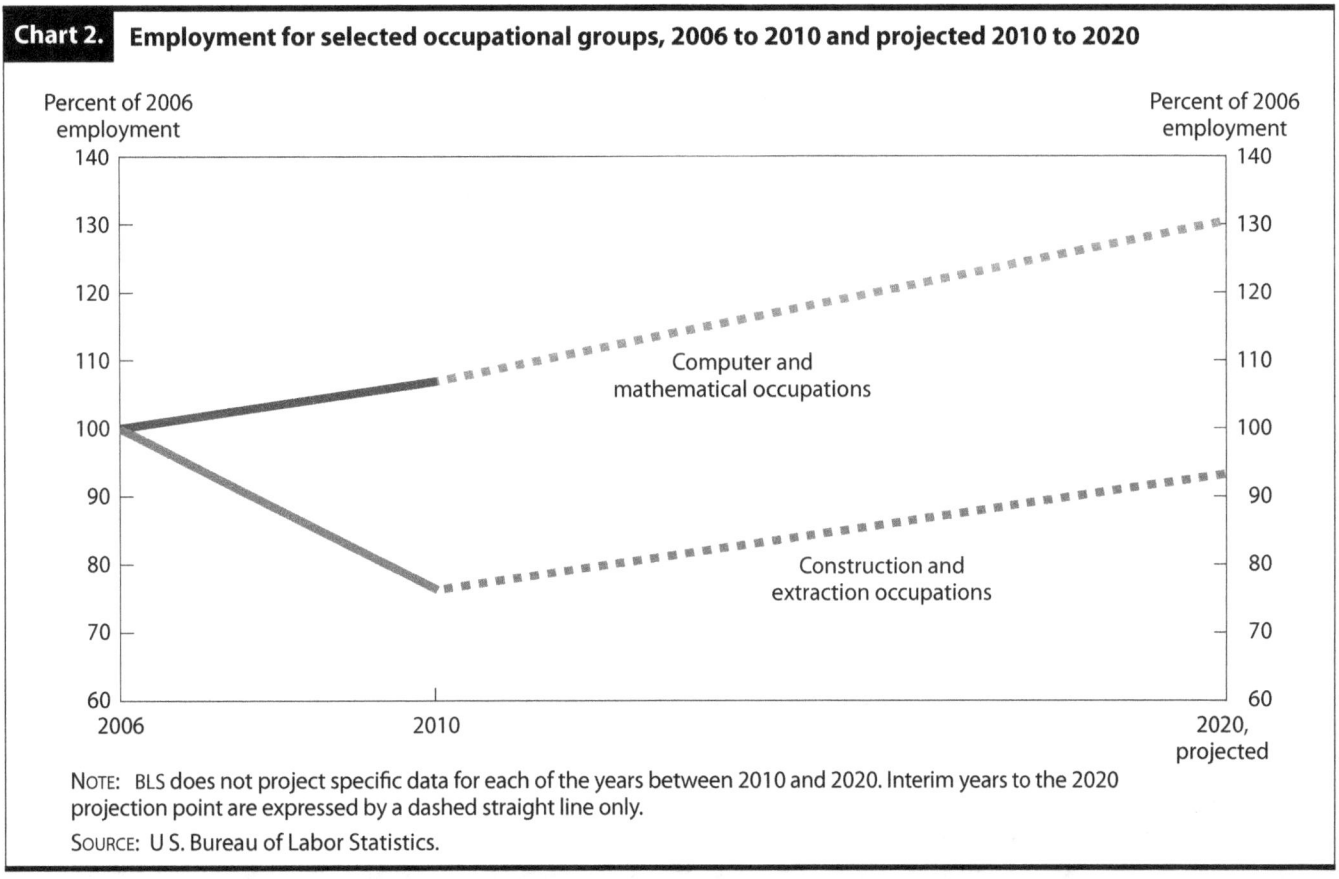

Chart 2. **Employment for selected occupational groups, 2006 to 2010 and projected 2010 to 2020**

Percent of 2006 employment

Percent of 2006 employment

Computer and mathematical occupations

Construction and extraction occupations

2006   2010   2020, projected

NOTE: BLS does not project specific data for each of the years between 2010 and 2020. Interim years to the 2020 projection point are expressed by a dashed straight line only.

SOURCE: U S. Bureau of Labor Statistics.

cles. Business and financial occupations are projected to grow more rapidly than several other occupations, indicating that the lack of growth from 2006 to 2010 may have resulted from the recession, with the fast projected growth including some recovery of lost potential growth.

Chart 5 shows occupational groups that grew by at least 2 percent from 2006 to 2010; all of these groups are projected to see continued growth through 2020. The two groups with the fastest growth from 2006 to 2010 were healthcare support occupations and healthcare practitioners and technical occupations. These two groups are projected to continue to see strong growth, adding a combined 3.5 million jobs from 2010 to 2020 after gaining 1.1 million from 2006 to 2010.

What follow are brief highlights about each of the major groups, discussed in the order the groups appear in the Standard Occupational Classification (SOC) system. The text table within each section shows, for that occupational group, the occupation that is projected to have the largest growth in number of jobs, the fastest growing and fastest declining (or slowest growing) occupations, and the occupation with the highest median annual wage in May 2010.

Management occupations.

Most new jobs:	
Construction managers	+86,600
Fastest growing (in percent):	
Social and community service managers	+26.7
Fastest declining (in percent):	
Postmasters and mail superintendents	–27.8
Highest paying:	
Chief executives	$165,080

Management occupations are projected to add 615,800 new jobs between 2010 and 2020. This represents 7.0 percent growth from their 2010 employment level of 8.8 million. Management occupations are projected to be the third-slowest-growing occupational group but, because they have relatively high employment, will be near the middle of the pack (14th out of 22) in projected employment growth from 2010 to 2020. Although projected to be slow growing, this relatively stable occupational group did not experience any decline in employment from 2006 to 2010.

Farmers, ranchers, and other agricultural managers, part of the management occupations group, are projected to experience an employment decline of 96,100 between 2010

Chart 3. Employment, 2006 to 2010 and projected 2010 to 2020, for occupational groups whose employment declined 2006–2010

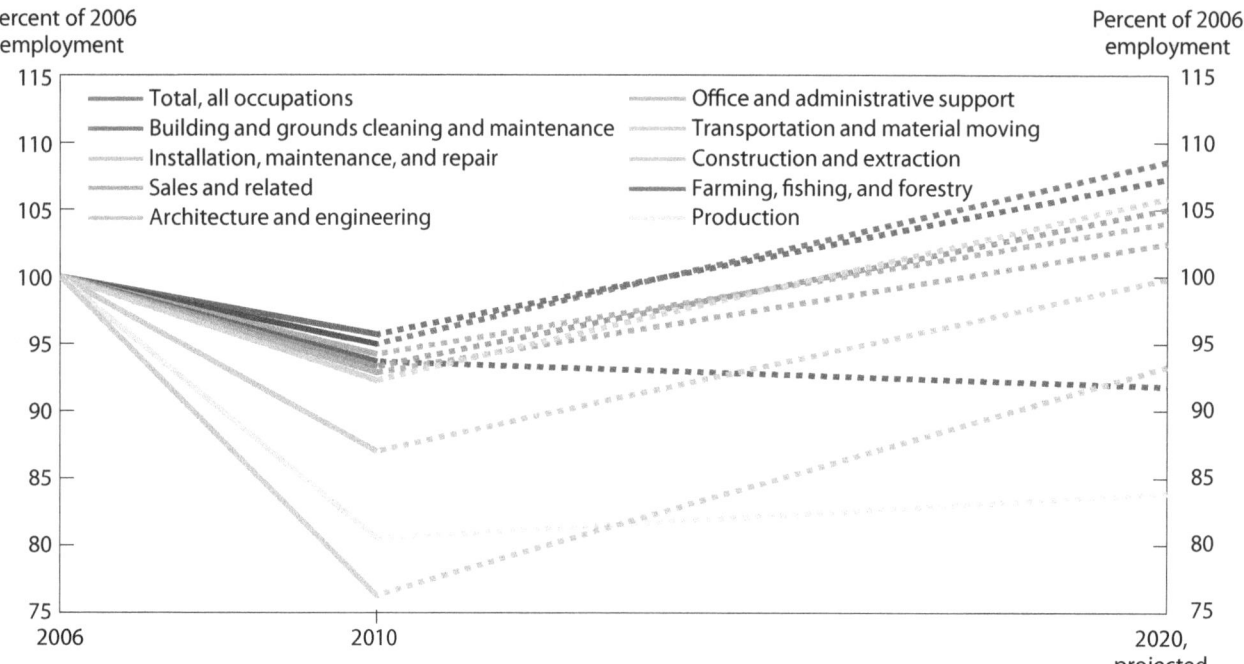

Percent of 2006 employment

Legend:
- Total, all occupations
- Building and grounds cleaning and maintenance
- Installation, maintenance, and repair
- Sales and related
- Architecture and engineering
- Office and administrative support
- Transportation and material moving
- Construction and extraction
- Farming, fishing, and forestry
- Production

2006   2010   2020, projected

NOTE: BLS does not project specific data for each of the years between 2010 and 2020. Interim years to the 2020 projection point are expressed by a dashed straight line only.

SOURCE: U.S. Bureau of Labor Statistics.

Chart 4. Employment, 2006 to 2010 and projected 2010 to 2020, for occupational groups with little employment change 2006–2010

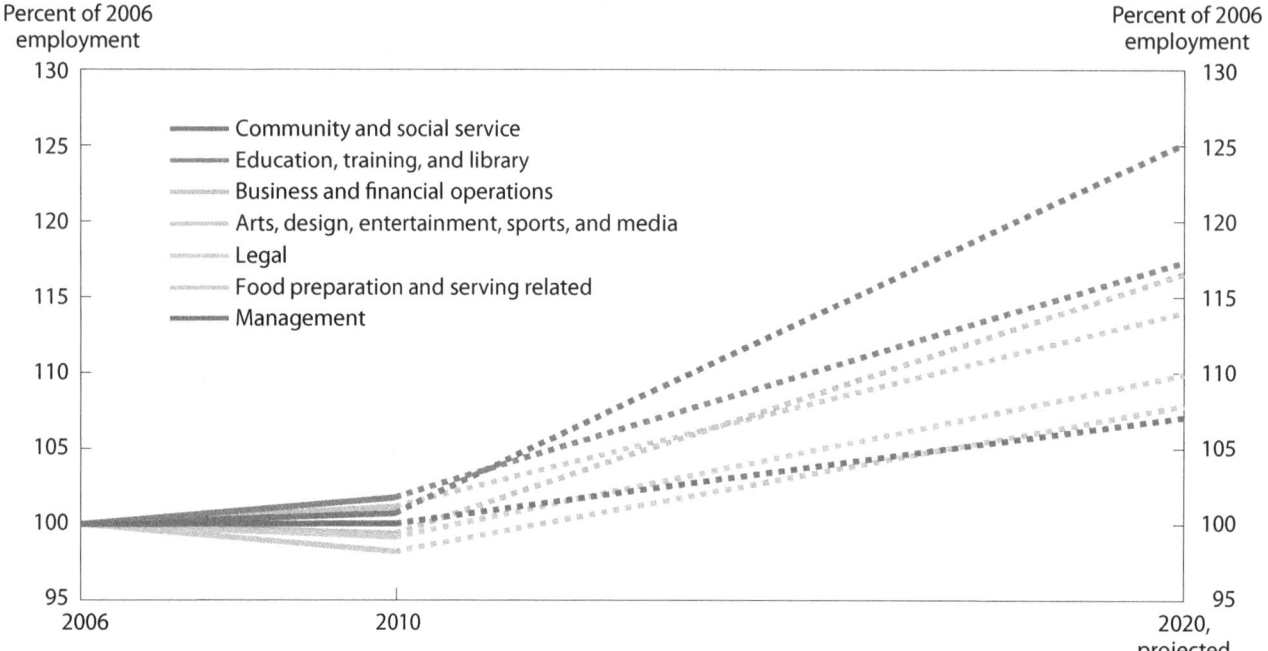

Percent of 2006 employment

Legend:
- Community and social service
- Education, training, and library
- Business and financial operations
- Arts, design, entertainment, sports, and media
- Legal
- Food preparation and serving related
- Management

2006   2010   2020, projected

NOTE: BLS does not project specific data for each of the years between 2010 and 2020. Interim years to the 2020 projection point are expressed by a dashed straight line only.

SOURCE: U.S. Bureau of Labor Statistics.

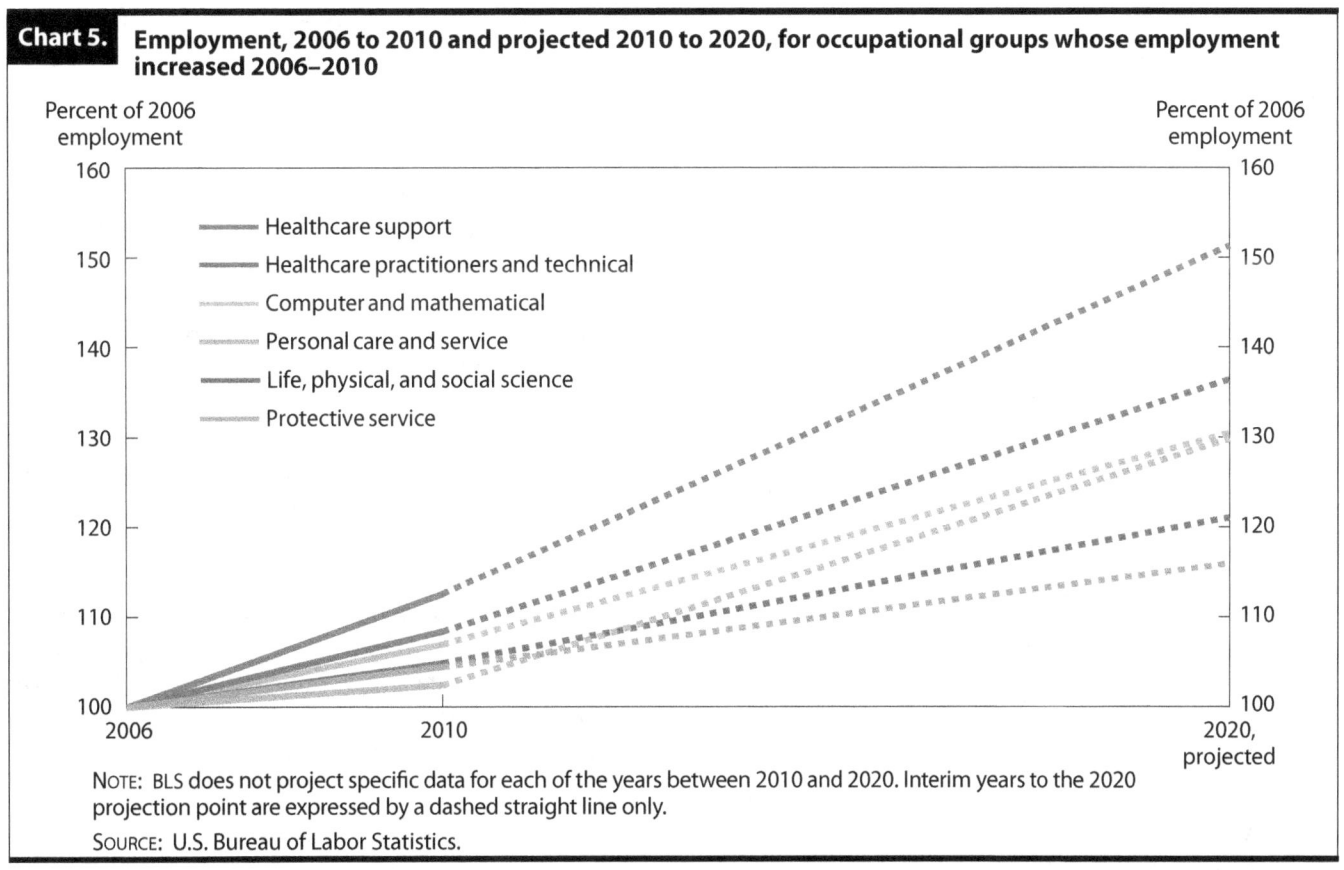

Chart 5. Employment, 2006 to 2010 and projected 2010 to 2020, for occupational groups whose employment increased 2006–2010

Percent of 2006 employment

Percent of 2006 employment

Legend:
- Healthcare support
- Healthcare practitioners and technical
- Computer and mathematical
- Personal care and service
- Life, physical, and social science
- Protective service

2006   2010   2020, projected

NOTE: BLS does not project specific data for each of the years between 2010 and 2020. Interim years to the 2020 projection point are expressed by a dashed straight line only.

SOURCE: U.S. Bureau of Labor Statistics.

and 2020. The job decline for farmers, ranchers, and other agricultural managers by itself slows the overall projected growth for this group by more than 1 percentage point. In addition, general and operations managers, who composed 20 percent of jobs in this group in 2010, are projected to grow by only 4.6 percent as these workers are overseeing increasingly larger areas of operation, causing their employment to grow slower than the industries in which they work.

Management occupations are found throughout all industries in the economy and tend to be high paying: their median annual wage of $91,440 was higher than for any other occupational group.[8] The high pay reflects, in part, the combination of formal postsecondary education and work experience that most of these occupations typically need.

Business and financial operations occupations.

Most new jobs:

Accountants and auditors	+190,700

Fastest growing (in percent):

Meeting, convention, and event planners	+43.7

Fastest declining (in percent):

Insurance appraisers, auto damage	−7.5

Highest paying:

Management analysts	$78,160

Business and financial operations occupations are projected to add 1.2 million new jobs as they grow by 17.3 percent between 2010 and 2020. This group includes business operations specialists—such as management analysts, human resources workers, and buyers and purchasing agents—and financial specialists—such as accountants and auditors, loan officers, and financial analysts. The business operations specialists group is larger (4.2 million vs. 2.6 million jobs for financial specialists in 2010), is projected to grow slightly faster (18.1 percent growth vs. 16.0 percent), and is projected to add more new jobs (751,400 vs. 421,100 new jobs) than financial operations occupations.

Business and financial operations workers are found in industries throughout the economy, but the largest numbers are found in government, professional and business services, and the finance and insurance industries. In these industries, business and financial operations occupations are projected to account for a larger share of industry employment in 2020 than in 2010, meaning the occupational group is expected to grow faster than the industry. Meeting, convention, and event planners, as well as market research analysts and marketing specialists, in particular, are expected to increase their share over that decade.

Computer and mathematical occupations.

Most new jobs:
Software developers, applications	+143,800
Fastest growing (in percent):	
Software developers, systems software	+32.4
Slowest growing (in percent):	
Mathematical technicians	+6.2
Highest paying:	
Computer and information research scientists	$100,600

Computer and mathematical occupations are projected to add 778,300 new jobs between 2010 and 2020, after having added 229,600 new jobs from 2006 to 2010. This represents 22.0 percent growth from 2010 to 2020, making the computer and mathematical occupational group the sixth-fastest-growing major occupational group. However, because it is a relatively small group, it ranks only twelfth (out of 22 groups) in the projected number of new jobs between 2010 and 2020.

Computer occupations are much larger than mathematical occupations, accounting for 3.4 million of the total 3.5 million jobs in computer and mathematical occupations in 2010. Employment in computer occupations also is projected to grow faster than mathematical occupations, with growth rates of 22.1 percent and 16.7 percent, respectively. Although computer occupations are found throughout the economy, fast growth in the computer systems design and related services industry is driving the growth in this group; this industry accounted for just over 20 percent of all jobs in computer occupations in 2010, but will generate more than half of all new computer jobs from 2010 to 2020.

Architecture and engineering occupations.

Most new jobs:
Civil engineers	+51,100
Fastest growing (in percent):	
Biomedical engineers	+61.7
Fastest declining (in percent):	
Aerospace engineering and operations technicians	−1.6
Highest paying:	
Petroleum engineers	$114,080

Architecture and engineering occupations are projected

to add 252,800 new jobs between 2010 and 2020 as they grow by 10.4 percent. This follows a decline of 149,800 jobs from 2006 to 2010. Engineers are the largest component of this major occupational group and will add the most new jobs, 160,400, but architects, surveyors, and cartographers are projected to grow faster, at 23.7 percent.

Nearly 30 percent of jobs for architecture and engineering occupations are found in manufacturing industries. The projected employment decline in many manufacturing industries is one of the main reasons this occupational group is projected to grow more slowly than other groups. Architecture and engineering jobs account for more than 20 percent of all jobs in the computer and electronic product manufacturing industry, so declines in this industry are expected to cause the loss of 33,900 jobs for occupations in this group.

Growth will come primarily from the architectural, engineering, and related services industry group. This industry group accounted for 26.4 percent of jobs for architecture and engineering occupations in 2010 but will contribute 173,700 new jobs for these occupations from 2010 to 2020, a growth rate of 27.0 percent.

Life, physical, and social science occupations.

Most new jobs:
Medical scientists, except epidemiologists	+36,400
Fastest growing (in percent):	
Medical scientists, except epidemiologists	+36.4
Fastest declining (in percent):	
Forest and conservation technicians	−1.0
Highest paying:	
Political scientists	$107,420

Life, physical, and social science occupations are projected to add 190,800 new jobs between 2010 and 2020 as they grow by 15.5 percent. Jobs for life scientists are projected to increase by 20.4 percent, making it the fastest growing of these three occupation groups. The employment of social scientists and related workers is projected to grow slightly slower, at 18.4 percent, while jobs for physical scientists are projected to grow by 12.7 percent.

Because workers in life, physical, and social science occupations do research, many of them are employed in scientific research and development services and in colleges, universities, and professional schools. These industries combine to employ more than a quarter of workers in life, physical, and social science occupations and are projected to account for almost one-third of all new jobs for this occupational group between 2010 and 2020.

Community and social service occupations.

Most new jobs:
Social and human service assistants   +106,000
Fastest growing (in percent):
Marriage and family therapists   +41.2
Slowest growing (in percent):
Directors, religious activities and education   +16.8
Highest paying:
Educational, guidance, school, and
  vocational counselors $53,380

Community and social service occupations include workers such as counselors, social workers, and religious workers. This occupational group is projected to add 582,300 new jobs between 2010 and 2020. This represents a 24.2-percent increase, making community and social service occupations the fourth-fastest-growing major occupational group. This group is unique in how uniform and fast the growth will be—each one of the 17 detailed occupations in this group is expected to grow faster than the 14.3-percent average growth rate for all occupations.

The individual and family services industry, despite employing only 11.9 percent of community and social service occupations, is projected to account for 26.5 percent of new jobs for this occupational group. The industry is projected to grow by more than 70 percent, giving many new opportunities to the community and social service occupations employed there, including social and human service assistants and child, family, and school social workers.

Legal occupations.

Most new jobs:
Lawyers   +73,600
Fastest growing (in percent):
Paralegals and legal assistants   +18.3
Fastest declining (in percent):
Title examiners, abstractors, and searchers   −1.4
Highest paying:
Judges, magistrates judges, and
  magistrates $119,270

Legal occupations are projected to add 131,000 new jobs between 2010 and 2020. This represents 10.8 percent growth from the occupational group's 2010 employment level of roughly 1.2 million. Legal occupations form the second-smallest major occupational group; it is expected to add the second-fewest new jobs. They tend to be high-paying jobs, though, with a median annual wage of $74,580 in May 2010.

Lawyers account for more than half of the jobs in this group, with employment of 728,200 in 2010. Because

their employment is growing at about the same rate as the group as a whole, the 73,600 new jobs projected for lawyers will also account for the majority of new jobs in the group.

Jobs for legal support workers are projected to grow 12.9 percent, which is somewhat faster than the group. However, they will only add 50,600 new jobs.

Education, training, and library occupations.

Most new jobs:
Postsecondary teachers   +113,600
Fastest growing (in percent):
Preschool teachers, except special
  education   +24.9
Slowest growing (in percent):
Career/technical education teachers,
  secondary school   +1.1
Highest paying:
Postsecondary teachers $62,050

The education, training, and library occupations group is projected to add 1.4 million new jobs, the sixth most of any major occupational group, with projected growth of 15.3 percent between 2010 and 2020. Of these new jobs, 655,000 will be for preschool, primary, secondary, and special education teachers, as this group is expected to grow by 15.0 percent, while another 305,700 jobs will be for postsecondary teachers, whose jobs are projected to increase 17.4 percent. Growth in education, training, and library occupations is influenced strongly by a rise in school enrollments. Enrollment in elementary and secondary schools tends to follow general population growth for children, while enrollment in postsecondary institutions is increasing faster than population growth as more high school graduates attend college and as members of the workforce seek additional education.

While the majority of education, training, and library jobs are located in public education, growth will be faster for these occupations in private elementary and secondary schools and private colleges, universities, and professional schools.

Arts, design, entertainment, sports, and media occupations.

Most new jobs:
Coaches and scouts   +71,400
Fastest growing (in percent):
Interpreters and translators   +42.2
Fastest declining (in percent):
Floral designers   −9.3
Highest paying:
Art directors $80,630

This diverse occupational group is projected to add 342,500 new jobs between 2010 and 2020, a growth rate of 12.6 percent. The group includes a variety of occupations:

- *Art and design workers*, such as graphic designers, merchandise displayers and window trimmers, and art directors.

- *Entertainers and performers, sports and related workers*, such as coaches and scouts, musicians and singers, producers and directors, music directors and composers, and actors.

- *Media and communication workers*, such as public relations specialists, writers and authors, editors, interpreters and translators, and reporters and correspondents.

- *Media and communication equipment workers*, such as photographers, audio and visual equipment technicians, broadcast technicians, and film and video editors.

The entertainers and performers, sports and related workers group is projected to grow the fastest, at 16.0 percent, and is also projected to add the most new jobs, 128,900. Jobs for media and communication workers are expected to grow by 106,100, while jobs for art and design workers will increase by 76,100.

Self-employed workers accounted for more than 30 percent of jobs in the arts, design, entertainment, sports, and media group in 2010. Jobs for the self-employed are projected to grow somewhat slower than wage and salary jobs, and are only projected to account for less than 20 percent of the new jobs for this occupational group.

Healthcare practitioners and technical occupations.

Most new jobs:

Registered nurses	+711,900
Fastest growing (in percent):	
Veterinary technologists and technicians	+52.0
Slowest growing (in percent):	
Respiratory therapy technicians	+4.1
Highest paying:	
Physicians and surgeons	≥$166,400

Healthcare practitioners and technical occupations are projected to add 2.0 million new jobs from 2010 to 2020, the second most of any major group. This follows an increase of 601,700 jobs from 2006 to 2010, more growth than any other occupational group. The healthcare practitioners and technical occupations growth rate of 25.9 percent from 2010 to 2020 is also the third fastest. This

group consists mainly of health diagnosing and treating practitioners—such as registered nurses, physicians and surgeons, and physical therapists—whose employment is projected to grow by 1.3 million, and health technologists and technicians—such as pharmacy technicians, emergency medical technicians and paramedics, and radiologic technologists and technicians—whose employment is projected to grow by 720,300.

The fast growth for the healthcare practitioners and technical occupational group is driven by increased spending on healthcare services, particularly by an aging population. Older individuals spend more on healthcare than those who are younger, so as the share of the population ages 65 and older grows, healthcare spending is expected to increase. The recently passed healthcare reform legislation could also have a large impact on the growth rate for healthcare practitioners, but its full effects remain unknown.

Healthcare support occupations.

Most new jobs:

Home health aides	+706,300
Fastest growing (in percent):	
Home health aides	+69.4
Slowest growing (in percent):	
Medical transcriptionists	+5.9
Highest paying:	
Occupational therapy assistants	$51,010

After having gained 466,500 new jobs from 2006 to 2010, the healthcare support occupations group is projected to be the fastest growing occupational group from 2010 to 2020, growing by 34.5 percent and creating 1.4 million more new jobs. About half, or 706,300, of these new jobs will be in a single occupation, home health aides, which is projected to grow by 69.4 percent. Home health aides accounted for 24 percent of this occupational group in 2010, but their proportion is projected to rise to 31 percent in 2020.

Much as it affects healthcare practitioners and technical occupations, an aging population that spends more on healthcare is a major factor behind the fast growth rate for healthcare support occupations. The recently passed healthcare reform legislation will also affect jobs within this occupation group, although the eventual impact is not known.

As with the more highly skilled healthcare practitioners and technical occupations, healthcare support occupations are concentrated within the health care industry—almost 80 percent of these jobs were in this industry in 2010. Together, the two groups account for more than 60 percent of jobs in this industry. Healthcare support occupations are more highly concentrated in ambulatory health care services, while healthcare practitioners and technical occupations are more highly concentrated in hospitals. Ambulatory health care services are projected to grow faster than hospitals, contributing to the projected faster growth for healthcare support occupations.

Protective service occupations.

Most new jobs:
Security guards +195,000
Fastest growing (in percent):
Private detectives and investigators +20.5
Slowest growing (in percent):
Crossing guards +1.1
Highest paying:
First-line supervisors of police and
   detectives $78,260

Protective service occupations are expected to add 364,500 new jobs—a growth rate of 11.0 percent. The majority of this occupational group consists of law enforcement workers, who predominantly work for governments, and security guards, who mostly work for private companies. About a third of the new jobs created will be in government, while another 40 percent will be in the investigation and security services industry.

Food preparation and serving related occupations.

Most new jobs:
Combined food preparation and
   serving workers, including fast food +398,000
Fastest growing (in percent):
Food servers, nonrestaurant +18.0
Fastest declining (in percent):
Cooks, fast food −3.6
Highest paying:
Chefs and head cooks $40,630

About 1.1 million new jobs will arise in the food preparation and serving related occupational group. Although this group was the third-largest major occupational group in 2010, it is growing at a slower-than-average rate of 9.8 percent and ranks only 10th in number of new jobs. More than half of the new jobs will be for food and beverage serving workers, such as waiters and waitresses. Employment of these workers is growing slightly faster (11.5 percent) than that of cooks and food preparation workers (8.6 percent), who account for most of the other jobs in this group.

Not surprisingly, the food preparation and serving related occupational group is highly concentrated in the food services and drinking places industry, where about three-quarters of these jobs are found, and the group accounts for 90 percent of all jobs in this industry. Faster growth for these jobs is found in the health care and social assistance industry, which accounted for 5 percent of jobs in 2010 but 11 percent of new jobs over the 2010-to-2020 period.

Building and grounds cleaning and maintenance occupations.

Most new jobs:
Janitors and cleaners, except maids
   and housekeeping cleaners +246,400
Fastest growing (in percent):
Pest control workers +26.1
Slowest growing (in percent):
First-line supervisors of housekeeping
   and janitorial workers +0.8
Highest paying:
First-line supervisors of landscaping, lawn
   service, and groundskeeping workers $41,860

This occupational group is projected to add 664,000 new jobs while growing at a slightly below-average rate (12.1 percent). This group includes, for example, janitors and landscaping workers. Jobs in almost all the occupations in this group typically need little to no education or training. As a result, they tend to be low-paying jobs, with a median annual wage of $22,490. About 14 percent of these workers were self-employed in 2010.

Jobs for grounds maintenance workers are projected to grow about twice as fast as jobs for building cleaning workers, but building cleaning workers are a larger occupational group and are projected to add more jobs—104,400 over the 10-year period.

Personal care and service occupations.

Most new jobs:
Personal care aides +607,000
Fastest growing (in percent):
Personal care aides +70.5
Fastest declining (in percent):
Motion picture projectionist −11.1
Highest paying:
Funeral service managers, directors,
   morticians, and undertakers $54,330

Personal care and service occupations are expected to grow by 26.8 percent, second fastest of all groups, as they add 1.3 million new jobs from 2010 to 2020. This group includes a wide variety of occupations, from child care workers to funeral attendants, manicurists to fitness trainers and aerobics instructors, and animal trainers to gaming dealers. Driving the overall growth in this group is personal care aides, the fastest growing occupation overall, which is projected to grow by 70.5 percent and add 607,000 new jobs. The fast growth in the number of elderly and their increasing desire to live in their own homes are the primary causes of the rapid expansion of this occupation. Personal care and service occupations tend to be low paid, with a median annual wage of $20,640 in May 2010.

Although just 24.2 percent of jobs in this occupational group were in the health care and social assistance industry in 2010, more than half of the new jobs through 2020 for this group will be in that industry. In contrast, the self-employed will account for only 12.8 percent of the group's new jobs, despite 22.0 percent of these workers being self-employed in 2010.

Sales and related occupations.

Most new jobs:
Retail salespersons   +706,800
Fastest growing (in percent):
Insurance sales agents   +21.9
Fastest declining (in percent):
Gaming change persons and booth cashiers   −12.1
Highest paying:
Sales engineers $87,390

Sales and related occupations are projected to add 1.9 million new jobs from 2010 to 2020 as this large occupational group grows at a slightly below-average 12.5-percent rate. This follows the loss of 1.1 million jobs from 2006 to 2010. More than half of the new jobs projected between 2010 and 2020 will be for retail sales workers, such as cashiers, whose employment is growing at about the same rate as the group as a whole. Faster growth, 17.8 percent, is expected for sales representatives, services, a group which is expected to add 272,100 new jobs.

In 2010, about 10 percent of jobs in sales and related occupations were for the self-employed, but jobs for self-employed sales and related workers are expected to decline over the projection period. Most new jobs will be found in the retail sales industry, where the majority of jobs in this group are currently found.

Office and administrative support occupations.

Most new jobs:
Office clerks, general   +489,500

Fastest growing (in percent):
Medical secretaries   +41.3
Fastest declining (in percent):
Postal service mail sorters, processors, and
    processing machine operators   −48.5
Highest paying:
Postal Service mail carriers $53,860

The largest occupational group, office and administrative support occupations comprised 22.6 million jobs in 2010 and are projected to add the most new jobs, 2.3 million through 2020, as the group grows by 10.3 percent. The majority of this job growth, however, represents a recovery of jobs lost during the recession; from 2006–2010, the employment of office and administrative support workers fell by 1.7 million. Office and administrative support occupations include information and records clerks, such as customer support representatives; secretaries and administrative assistants; financial clerks, such as billing and posting clerks; and material recording, scheduling, dispatching, and distributing workers, such as stock clerks and order fillers.

Occupations within this group have particularly varied growth rates. A number of occupations are declining because of automation, such as switchboard operators including answering service (−23.3 percent); file clerks (−4.8 percent); postal service mail sorters, processors, and processing machine operators (−48.5 percent); and data entry keyers (−6.8 percent). Others are growing rapidly, such as medical secretaries (41.3 percent), cargo and freight agents (29.3 percent), and receptionists and information clerks (23.7 percent).

The occupations within this group are found throughout the economy, and the number of new jobs varies greatly by industry. More than one-third of the new jobs will arise in the health care and social assistance industry, even though this industry accounted for only 12.2 percent of office and administrative support jobs in 2010. On the other hand, in government there will be a decline of 128,000 jobs for occupations in this group through 2020.

Farming, fishing, and forestry occupations.

Most new jobs:
Logging equipment operators   +1,300
Fastest growing (in percent):
Log graders and scalers   +13.3
Fastest declining (in percent):
Animal breeders   −7.5
Highest paying:
First-line supervisors of farming, fishing,
    and forestry workers $41,800

The smallest major occupational group in 2010 was farming, fishing, and forestry occupations, which had only 972,100 jobs. It is also the only declining group, projected to lose 19,400 jobs, or 2.0 percent, through 2020. Agricultural workers, who accounted for 85 percent of all jobs in this group in 2010, are projected to lose 19,100 jobs. Fishing and hunting workers are expected to lose 2,000 jobs, while forest, conservation, and logging workers will gain 2,400 jobs. Three-quarters of farming, fishing, and forestry occupation jobs are located in the declining agriculture, forestry, fishing, and hunting industry sector; jobs for occupations in this group account for over half of all jobs in this industry.

Construction and extraction occupations.

Most new jobs:	
Construction laborers	+212,400
Fastest growing (in percent):	
Helpers—brickmasons, blockmasons, stonemasons, and tile and marble setters	+60.1
Slowest growing (in percent):	
Explosive workers, ordnance handling experts, and blasters	+0.2
Highest paying:	
Elevator installers and repairers	$70,910

Construction and extraction occupations are projected to add about 1.4 million new jobs over the 2010–2020 period as their employment grows by 22.2 percent. This fast growth rate will not result in a full recovery from the recent recession, however, which caused the loss of 2.0 million jobs from 2006 to 2010 for this group. Construction trades workers, such as carpenters and electricians, will account for 1.1 million of the new jobs. Jobs for extraction workers, who work in the mining and oil and gas industries, are expected to grow much slower (6.9 percent) than construction trades and will increase by only 15,500. Most workers in construction and extraction occupations typically need little formal education for their jobs, but they tend to receive significant on-the-job training. The median annual wage of $39,080 for construction and extraction occupations in May 2010 is higher than the average for all occupations.

The majority of construction and extraction occupation jobs were in the fast-growing construction industry, which is expected to account for 1.2 million of the new jobs in this group. A fifth of jobs were for self-employed workers in 2010, but jobs for the self-employed are projected to grow by only 5.8 percent, resulting in 75,400 new jobs.

Installation, maintenance, and repair occupations.

Most new jobs:	
Maintenance and repair workers, general	+142,000
Fastest growing (in percent):	
Bicycle repairers	+37.6
Fastest declining (in percent):	
Fabric menders, except garment	−6.3
Highest paying:	
Electrical and electronics repairers, powerhouse, substation, and relay	$65,230

About 800,200 new jobs are projected in installation, maintenance, and repair occupations between 2010 and 2020, a growth rate of 14.7 percent. This group lost about 454,700 jobs from 2006 to 2010, so a little more than half of the projected increase is making up for job losses during the period that included the recession. Vehicle and mobile equipment mechanics, installers, and repairers–such as automotive service technicians and mechanics–will account for 267,300 new jobs, while electrical and electronic equipment mechanics, installers, and repairers–such as security and fire alarm systems installers–will account for 71,800 new jobs.

Almost one-quarter of the new jobs are expected to be in the construction industry, where jobs for installation, maintenance, and repair occupations are projected to grow by 40.6 percent. In contrast, employment of installation, maintenance, and repair occupations in the manufacturing industry is projected to grow by only 4.0 percent over the decade.

Production occupations.

Most new jobs:	
Team assemblers	+52,300
Fastest growing (in percent):	
Sawing machine setters, operators, and tenders, wood	+24.7
Fastest declining (in percent):	
Shoe machine operators and tenders	−53.4
Highest paying:	
Nuclear power reactor operators	$75,650

Production occupations are projected to add 356,800 new jobs, resulting from a slower-than-average 4.2-percent growth rate. This growth is dwarfed by the 2.1 million jobs that were lost in this group from 2006 to 2010 as the manufacturing sector was hard hit by the recession. Although production workers are heavily concentrated in the manufacturing industry, only 48,800 new jobs for these occupations are expected for this industry.

In contrast, 127,800 new jobs are expected in the employment services industry, as manufacturers increasingly use workers from temporary help services.

Most minor groups within production occupations, such as assemblers and fabricators or metal workers and plastic workers, are growing at single-digit rates, comparable to the group as a whole. However, jobs for textile, apparel, and furnishings workers are projected to decline by 9.6 percent, resulting in the loss of 65,500 jobs. In contrast, jobs for woodworkers are projected to grow by 17.1 percent, adding 40,200 jobs.

Transportation and material moving occupations.

Most new jobs:
Heavy and tractor-trailer truck drivers   +330,100
Fastest growing (in percent):
Ambulance drivers and attendants, except
    emergency medical technicians   +32.1
Fastest declining (in percent):
Gas compressor and gas pumping station
    operators   −10.1
Highest paying:
Air traffic controllers $108,040

Transportation and material moving occupations are projected to add 1.3 million new jobs, reflecting 14.8-percent growth from 2010 to 2020. This growth matches the 1.3 million jobs that were lost from 2006 to 2010. Nearly all the projected new jobs from 2010 to 2020 will be for motor vehicle operators (such as truck drivers), who will add 641,100 jobs, and for material moving workers (such as packers and packagers, hand), who will add 552,600 jobs.

Almost half of the new jobs for this group will be found in the transportation and warehousing industry, even though this industry accounted for only 28.8 percent of the group in 2010. This is because jobs for material moving occupations are growing quickly, at 22.1 percent, in this industry. The retail trade and wholesale trade industries will also contribute 131,100 and 164,600 new transportation and material moving jobs, respectively.

Detailed occupations

Table 2 lists the 30 occupations with the largest projected percentage employment increases from 2010 to 2020. The increase in healthcare employment is reflected here as 10 of the 30 occupations shown are in either the healthcare practitioner and technical occupations group or the healthcare support occupations group. Construction and extraction occupations, which are projected to grow as the construction industry begins to recover from the recent recession, account for 8 of the 30 occupations. The 30 occupations are relatively evenly distributed in terms of typical education needed for entry. (The education classification system is described in more detail in the last section of this article). A bachelor's or graduate degree is needed for 12 of the occupations, while 5 need an associate's degree, and 13 need a high school diploma or less. However, four of the construction occupations typically need, in addition to a high school diploma, formal apprenticeship training; these are reinforcing iron and rebar workers, glaziers, brickmasons and blockmasons, and stonemasons.

The two fastest growing occupations, personal care aides and home health aides, will be affected by demographic changes. Workers in both occupations assist the elderly, persons with disabilities, and convalescents in the person's home or in a care facility. Home health aides provide health services, such as administering medications, while personal care aides provide general services, such as cooking meals. The growing elderly population will require some care and assistance in their own homes or health care facilities, which should lead to increased demand for these occupations.

Table 3 lists the 30 occupations with the largest projected numeric job increases from 2010 to 2020. These are generally larger occupations that will account for many new jobs even though some of these occupations are projected to grow at average rates. The expected growth in healthcare will drive the demand for the six the occupations on this list in either the healthcare practitioner and technical occupations or healthcare support occupations groups, including registered nurses, which are projected to add the most new jobs. Six office and administrative support occupations appear on this list as well, primarily because they are large occupations that are employed across many industries. Five of these six had more than a million jobs in 2010, while the sixth occupation, medical secretaries, is expected to grow rapidly because of its concentration in the fast-growing health care industry. In contrast with the fastest growing occupations, the occupations with the largest numeric increases tend to have lower education needs. A high school diploma or less is sufficient to enter 23 of the occupations, while a bachelor's or higher degree is the typical level needed to enter only 4 of the occupations on this list.

Tables 4 and 5 show the 10 occupations with the largest percentage declines and the largest numeric declines in employment, respectively. Four occupations appear on both lists, making for 16 unique occupations. Five of these

Table 2. Employment and wages of occupations with the largest percentage growth in jobs, 2010 and projected 2020

(Numbers in thousands)

Matrix code	2010 National Employment Matrix title	Employment		Projected change, 2010–2020		Median annual wage, May 2010[1]	Typical education needed for entry
		2010	2020	Number	Percent		
00–0000	Total, all occupations	143,068.1	163,537.1	20,468.9	14.3	$33,840	—
39–9021	Personal care aides	861.0	1,468.0	607.0	70.5	19,640	Less than high school
31–1011	Home health aides	1,017.7	1,723.9	706.3	69.4	20,560	Less than high school
17–2031	Biomedical engineers	15.7	25.4	9.7	61.7	81,540	Bachelor's degree
47–3011	Helpers—brickmasons, blockmasons, stonemasons, and tile and marble setters	29.4	47.0	17.6	60.1	27,780	Less than high school
47–3012	Helpers—carpenters	46.5	72.4	25.9	55.7	25,760	Less than high school
29–2056	Veterinary technologists and technicians	80.2	121.9	41.7	52.0	29,710	Associate's degree
47–2171	Reinforcing iron and rebar workers	19.1	28.4	9.3	48.6	38,430	High school diploma or equivalent
31–2021	Physical therapist assistants	67.4	98.2	30.8	45.7	49,690	Associate's degree
47–3015	Helpers—pipelayers, plumbers, pipefitters, and steamfitters	57.9	84.2	26.3	45.4	26,740	High school diploma or equivalent
13–1121	Meeting, convention, and event planners	71.6	102.9	31.3	43.7	45,260	Bachelor's degree
29–2032	Diagnostic medical sonographers	53.7	77.1	23.4	43.5	64,380	Associate's degree
31–2011	Occupational therapy assistants	28.5	40.8	12.3	43.3	51,010	Associate's degree
31–2022	Physical therapist aides	47.0	67.3	20.3	43.1	23,680	High school diploma or equivalent
47–2121	Glaziers	41.9	59.6	17.7	42.4	36,640	High school diploma or equivalent
27–3091	Interpreters and translators	58.4	83.1	24.6	42.2	43,300	Bachelor's degree
43–6013	Medical secretaries	508.7	718.9	210.2	41.3	30,530	High school diploma or equivalent
13–1161	Market research analysts and marketing specialists	282.7	399.3	116.6	41.2	60,570	Bachelor's degree
21–1013	Marriage and family therapists	36.0	50.8	14.8	41.2	45,720	Master's degree
47–2021	Brickmasons and blockmasons	89.2	125.3	36.1	40.5	46,930	High school diploma or equivalent
29–1123	Physical therapists	198.6	276.0	77.4	39.0	76,310	Doctoral or professional degree
29–2021	Dental hygienists	181.8	250.3	68.5	37.7	68,250	Associate's degree
49–3091	Bicycle repairers	9.9	13.6	3.7	37.6	23,660	High school diploma or equivalent
29–1181	Audiologists	13.0	17.8	4.8	36.8	66,660	Doctoral or professional degree
21–1091	Health educators	63.4	86.6	23.2	36.5	45,830	Bachelor's degree
47–2022	Stonemasons	15.6	21.4	5.7	36.5	37,180	High school diploma or equivalent
13–1051	Cost estimators	185.4	252.9	67.5	36.4	57,860	Bachelor's degree
19–1042	Medical scientists, except epidemiologists	100.0	136.5	36.4	36.4	76,700	Doctoral or professional degree
21–1014	Mental health counselors	120.3	163.9	43.6	36.3	38,150	Master's degree
47–2072	Pile-driver operators	4.1	5.6	1.5	36.0	47,860	High school diploma or equivalent
29–1131	Veterinarians	61.4	83.4	22.0	35.9	82,040	Doctoral or professional degree

[1] For wage and salary workers, from the Occupational Employment Statistics survey.   SOURCE: U.S. Bureau of Labor Statistics.

occupations are textile, apparel, or furnishings workers, all concentrated in textile and apparel manufacturing industries, which are declining rapidly because of increased imports. Four occupations related to the postal service make the lists as that agency cuts costs and jobs in the face of operating deficits. The occupation expected to decline the fastest, at 53.4 percent, is shoe machine operators and tenders. However, this decline will only cause the loss of 1,700 jobs over the 10-year period because of the occupa-

tion's small size. Farmers, ranchers, and other agricultural managers will lose 96,100 jobs, more than any other occupation, as technological improvements and consolidation continue to reduce the number of workers needed to produce the nation's food. Nearly all the occupations in tables 4 and 5 typically need no more than a high school diploma for entry. The only exception is semiconductor processors, for which an associate's degree is the typical education needed for entry.

Table 3. **Employment and wages of occupations with the largest numeric growth in jobs, 2010 and projected 2020**

(Numbers in thousands)

Matrix code	2010 National Employment Matrix title	Employment		Projected change, 2010–2020		Median annual wage, May 2010[1]	Typical education needed for entry
		2010	2020	Number	Percent		
00–0000	Total, all occupations	143,068.2	163,537.1	20,468.9	14.3	$33,840	—
29–1111	Registered nurses	2,737.4	3,449.3	711.9	26.0	64,690	Associate's degree
41–2031	Retail salespersons	4,261.6	4,968.4	706.8	16.6	20,670	Less than high school
31–1011	Home health aides	1,017.7	1,723.9	706.3	69.4	20,560	Less than high school
39–9021	Personal care aides	861.0	1,468.0	607.0	70.5	19,640	Less than high school
43–9061	Office clerks, general	2,950.7	3,440.2	489.5	16.6	26,610	High school diploma or equivalent
35–3021	Combined food preparation and serving workers, including fast food	2,682.1	3,080.1	398.0	14.8	17,950	Less than high school
43–4051	Customer service representatives	2,187.3	2,525.6	338.4	15.5	30,460	High school diploma or equivalent
53–3032	Heavy and tractor-trailer truck drivers	1,604.8	1,934.9	330.1	20.6	37,770	High school diploma or equivalent
53–7062	Laborers and freight, stock, and material movers, hand	2,068.2	2,387.3	319.1	15.4	23,460	Less than high school
25–1000	Postsecondary teachers	1,756.0	2,061.7	305.7	17.4	45,690	Doctoral or professional degree
31–1012	Nursing aides, orderlies, and attendants	1,505.3	1,807.2	302.0	20.1	24,010	Postsecondary nondegree award
39–9011	Childcare workers	1,282.3	1,544.3	262.0	20.4	19,300	High school diploma or equivalent
43–3031	Bookkeeping, accounting, and auditing clerks	1,898.3	2,157.4	259.0	13.6	34,030	High school diploma or equivalent
41–2011	Cashiers	3,362.6	3,612.8	250.2	7.4	18,500	Less than high school
25–2021	Elementary school teachers, except special education	1,476.5	1,725.3	248.8	16.8	51,660	Bachelor's degree
43–4171	Receptionists and information clerks	1,048.5	1,297.0	248.5	23.7	25,240	High school diploma or equivalent
37–2011	Janitors and cleaners, except maids and housekeeping cleaners	2,310.4	2,556.8	246.4	10.7	22,210	Less than high school
37–3011	Landscaping and groundskeeping workers	1,151.5	1,392.3	240.8	20.9	23,400	Less than high school
41–4012	Sales representatives, wholesale and manufacturing, except technical and scientific products	1,430.0	1,653.4	223.4	15.6	52,440	High school diploma or equivalent
47–2061	Construction laborers	998.8	1,211.2	212.4	21.3	29,280	Less than high school
43–6013	Medical secretaries	508.7	718.9	210.2	41.3	30,530	High school diploma or equivalent
43–1011	First-line supervisors of office and administrative support workers	1,424.4	1,627.8	203.4	14.3	47,460	High school diploma or equivalent
47–2031	Carpenters	1,001.7	1,197.6	196.0	19.6	39,530	High school diploma or equivalent
35–3031	Waiters and waitresses	2,260.3	2,456.2	195.9	8.7	18,330	Less than high school
33–9032	Security guards	1,035.7	1,230.7	195.0	18.8	23,920	High school diploma or equivalent
25–9041	Teacher assistants	1,288.30	1,479.30	191.1	14.8	23,220	High school diploma or equivalent
13–2011	Accountants and auditors	1,216.90	1,407.60	190.7	15.7	61,690	Bachelor's degree
29–2061	Licensed practical and licensed vocational nurses	752.3	920.8	168.5	22.4	40,380	Postsecondary nondegree award
29–1060	Physicians and surgeons	691	859.3	168.3	24.4	111,570	Doctoral or professional degree
31–9092	Medical assistants	527.6	690.4	162.9	30.9	28,860	High school diploma or equivalent

[1] For wage and salary workers, from the Occupational Employment Statistics survey.

SOURCE: U.S. Bureau of Labor Statistics.

Job openings from replacement needs

New jobs account for only a portion of all jobs that are expected to be available during the projection period. Many workers will retire, leave the labor force, or transfer to other occupations, creating additional opportunities for workers to enter each occupation. These replacement needs, when added to new jobs, create a more complete picture of job openings. While projections of job growth and decline provide the best picture of how occupational

Table 4. Employment and wages of occupations with the largest percentage decline in jobs, 2010 and projected 2020

(Numbers in thousands)

Matrix code	2010 National Employment Matrix title	Employment		Projected change, 2010–2020		Median annual wage, May 2010[1]	Typical education needed for entry
		2010	2020	Number	Percent		
00–0000	Total, all occupations	143,068.2	163,537.1	20,468.9	14.3	$33,840	—
51–6042	Shoe machine operators and tenders	3.2	1.5	–1.7	–53.4	26,280	High school diploma or equivalent
43–5053	Postal service mail sorters, processors, and processing machine operators	142.0	73.0	–68.9	–48.5	53,080	High school diploma or equivalent
43–5051	Postal service clerks	65.6	34.0	–31.6	–48.2	53,100	High school diploma or equivalent
51–6092	Fabric and apparel patternmakers	6.0	3.9	–2.1	–35.6	38,970	High school diploma or equivalent
11–9131	Postmasters and mail superintendents	24.5	17.7	–6.8	–27.8	60,300	High school diploma or equivalent
51–6031	Sewing machine operators	163.2	121.1	–42.1	–25.8	20,600	Less than high school
43–2011	Switchboard operators, including answering service	142.5	109.3	–33.2	–23.3	24,920	High school diploma or equivalent
51–6062	Textile cutting machine setters, operators, and tenders	14.9	11.7	–3.3	–21.8	23,490	High school diploma or equivalent
51–6063	Textile knitting and weaving machine setters, operators, and tenders	22.5	18.4	–4.1	–18.2	25,870	High school diploma or equivalent
51–9141	Semiconductor processors	21.1	17.3	–3.8	–17.9	33,130	Associate's degree

[1] For wage and salary workers, from the Occupational Employment Statistics survey.
SOURCE: U.S. Bureau of Labor Statistics.

Table 5. Employment and wages of occupations with the largest numeric decline in jobs, 2010 and projected 2020

(Numbers in thousands)

Matrix code	2010 National Employment Matrix title	Employment		Projected change, 2010–2020		Median annual wage, May 2010[1]	Typical education needed for entry
		2010	2020	Number	Percent		
00–0000	Total, all occupations	143,068.2	163,537.1	20,468.9	14.3	$33,840	—
11–9013	Farmers, ranchers, and other agricultural managers	1,202.5	1,106.4	–96.1	–8.0	60,750	High school diploma or equivalent
43–5053	Postal service mail sorters, processors, and processing machine operators	142.0	73.0	–68.9	–48.5	53,080	High school diploma or equivalent
51–6031	Sewing machine operators	163.2	121.1	–42.1	–25.8	20,600	Less than high school
43–5052	Postal service mail carriers	316.7	278.5	–38.1	–12.0	53,860	High school diploma or equivalent
43–2011	Switchboard operators, including answering service	142.5	109.3	–33.2	–23.3	24,920	High school diploma or equivalent
43–5051	Postal service clerks	65.6	34.0	–31.6	–48.2	53,100	High school diploma or equivalent
35–2011	Cooks, fast food	530.4	511.4	–19.1	–3.6	18,100	Less than high school
45–2090	Miscellaneous agricultural workers	746.4	727.3	–19.1	–2.6	19,180	Less than high school
43–9021	Data entry keyers	234.7	218.8	–15.9	–6.8	27,450	High school diploma or equivalent
43–9022	Word processors and typists	115.3	102.1	–13.2	–11.5	33,400	High school diploma or equivalent

[1] For wage and salary workers, from the Occupational Employment Statistics survey.
SOURCE: U.S. Bureau of Labor Statistics.

employment is expected to change, job openings provide a better description of the labor market that new entrants will face. Projections of job openings also serve as an estimate of the minimum number of workers who will need to be trained for occupations that require pre-employment education or training.[9]

From 2010 to 2020, about 33.7 million job openings are expected to come from replacement needs, compared with 21.1 million job openings from growth.[10] In four out of five occupations, openings due to replacement needs exceed the number due to growth. Occupations where more openings are due to growth tend to be those that are growing the fastest. For example, personal care aides, the fastest growing occupation, will add 607,000 jobs because of growth, but only 68,200 because of replacement needs.

Occupations that have low formal educational requirements and that are often taken as temporary positions have some of the highest replacement needs. For example, there will be 1.5 million openings for cashiers due to the need to replace workers who leave the occupation, far more than the 250,200 jobs that will arise because of growth. Waiters and waitresses will have 1.1 million job openings due to replacement needs, compared with 195,900 due to growth.

Job openings due to replacement needs occur even in declining occupations. Although employment of farmers, ranchers, and other agricultural managers is expected to decline by 96,100 jobs, there will be 234,500 job openings due to the need to replace workers who leave this occupation.

Job outlook by education

BLS is releasing a new education and training classification system with the 2010–2020 projections that assigns three classifications to each occupation: typical education needed for entry, work experience in a related occupation commonly considered necessary to be hired, and typical on-the-job training needed to attain competency in an occupation. (See box on next pages.) This new system was developed primarily for career exploration purposes but is also useful in depicting projected trends for occupations grouped by the type of preparation and experience needed for entry and attaining competency. A forthcoming article in the *Monthly Labor Review* will examine the system in more detail; included here are a few highlights of the new system.

Table 6 presents the employment projections for occupations on the basis of the new education classifications. BLS makes projections by occupation, not education level, so the data here represent the 2010 and projected 2020 employment for occupations assigned to each category. This is not the same as a projection of the number of workers with each of these education levels. Workers may have educational attainment that is either higher or lower than what is typically needed for entry into the occupation in which they are employed.[11]

The fastest growth is projected in occupations assigned to the master's degree level; these occupations are projected to grow by 21.7 percent. All six categories of occupations that typically need some postsecondary education are expected to grow faster than the average for all occupations, while those occupations assigned to the high school or less-than-high-school categories will grow slower than the average. However, 62.6 percent of new jobs and 69.2 percent of job openings due to growth and

replacement needs are expected to arise in occupations assigned to these two lowest education categories; these occupations accounted for 69.3 percent of all jobs in 2010.

Wages are much higher in the categories of bachelor's degree, master's degree, and doctoral or professional degree, with median annual wages above $60,000 in all three categories. The median annual wage is also above $60,000 for occupations in the associate's degree category; however, wages are considerably less for workers with jobs that typically need less than an associate's degree. Occupations assigned to the postsecondary nondegree award and the high school diploma or equivalent categories have median wages around $34,000, while wages in the less-than-high-school category are only about $20,000.

An important feature of the new education and training classification system is that it allows examination of projected employment trends across all three dimensions of preparation: entry-level education, work experience in a related occupation, and on-the-job training. For example, in 2010, 43.5 percent of all jobs were in occupations assigned to the high school diploma or equivalent category. However, not all occupations that typically need a high school diploma need the same type of on-the-job training. Chart 6 shows data for occupations that typically need a high school diploma or equivalent for entry, broken down by the typical on-the-job training needed to attain competency in the occupation. Occupations that need short- and moderate-term on-the-job training account for 68.8 percent of the 2010 employment in occupations that need high school or equivalent education for entry and account for the majority of new jobs projected for these occupations. However, jobs in high school diploma occupations that typically receive training through an apprenticeship are expected to grow by 22.5 percent, almost twice as fast as the average for all high school diploma occupations. Apprenticeship occupations have a higher median annual wage in 2010 ($44,430) than the high school occupations that typically need short-term ($28,420) or moderate-term ($34,750) on-the-job training.

Jobs in occupations that need a high school diploma are spread more evenly among training categories than are jobs in occupations that typically need less than high school. As chart 7 shows, more than 90 percent of the jobs in occupations that typically need less than a high school diploma are in occupations that have only short-term on-the-job training. The relatively low skill level of these occupations, both in terms of formal education and on-the-job training, is reflected in the low median annual wage ($20,070 for less than high school occupations), as noted earlier. (See table 6.)

Definitions for the education and training classification system

The Bureau of Labor Statistics (BLS) education and training classification system consists of three categories of information that BLS analysts have assigned to each detailed occupation in the 2010–2020 National Employment Matrix. The categories are

- typical education needed for entry,
- commonly required work experience in a related occupation, and
- typical on-the-job training needed to obtain competency in the occupation.

Each category and its related choice selections are defined below. This education and training system replaces the one used for the 2008–2018 projections cycle.

Typical education needed for entry

This category best describes the typical level of education that most workers need to enter the occupation. Occupations are assigned one of the following eight education levels:

Doctoral or professional degree. Completion of a doctoral degree (Ph.D.) usually requires at least 3 years of full-time academic work beyond a bachelor's degree. Completion of a professional degree usually requires at least 3 years of full-time academic study beyond a bachelor's degree. Examples of occupations for which a professional degree is the typical form of entry-level education include lawyers, physicians and surgeons, and dentists.

Master's degree. Completion of this degree usually requires 1 or 2 years of full-time academic study beyond a bachelor's degree. Examples of occupations in this category include statisticians, physician assistants, and educational, vocational, and school counselors.

Bachelor's degree. Completion of this degree generally requires at least 4 years, but not more than 5 years, of full-time academic study beyond high school. Examples of occupations in this category include budget analysts, dietitians, and civil engineers.

Associate's degree. Completion of this degree usually requires at least 2 years but not more than 4 years of full-time academic study beyond high school. Examples of occupations in this category include mechanical drafters, respiratory therapists, and dental hygienists.

Postsecondary nondegree award. These programs lead to a certificate or other award but not a degree. The certificate is awarded by the educational institution and is the result of completing formal postsecondary schooling. Certification, which is issued by a professional organization or certifying body, is not included here. Some postsecondary nondegree award programs last only a few weeks, while others may last 1 to 2 years. Examples of occupations in this category include nursing aides, emergency medical technicians (EMTs) and paramedics, and hairstylists.

Some college, no degree. This category signifies the achievement of a high school diploma or equivalent plus the completion of one or more postsecondary courses that did not result in a degree or award. Examples of occupations in this category are actors and computer support specialists.

High school diploma or equivalent. This category signifies the completion of high school or an equivalent program resulting in the award of a high school diploma or an equivalent, such as the General Educational Development (GED) credential. Examples of occupations in this category include social and human service assistants and pharmacy technicians.

Less than high school. This category signifies the completion of any level of primary or secondary education that did not result in the award of a high school diploma or an equivalent. Examples of occupations in this category include janitors and cleaners, cashiers, and carpet installers.

Work experience in a related occupation

For some occupations, work experience in a related occupation may be a typical method of entry. The majority of occupations in this category are first-line supervisors or managers of service, sales, and production occupations. Although work experience in a related occupation is beneficial for all occupations, this metric is meant to capture work experience that is commonly considered necessary by employers or is a commonly accepted substitute for other, more formal types of training or education. Occupations are assigned one of the following four categories that deal with length of time spent gaining related work experience:

More than 5 years. This is assigned to occupations if more than 5 years of work experience in a related occupation is typically needed for entry. Examples include construction managers and computer and information systems managers.

1 to 5 years. To enter occupations in this category, workers typically need 1–5 years of work experience in a related occupation. Examples include marketing managers and database administrators.

Less than 1 year. Examples of occupations that typically require less than 1 year of work experience in a related occupation include restaurant cooks and industrial truck and tractor operators.

None. No work experience in a related occupation is typically required. Examples are audiologists and actuaries.

Typical on-the-job training needed to attain competency in the occupation

This category encompasses any additional training or preparation that is typically needed, once a person is employed in an occupation, to attain competency in the skills needed in that occupation. Training is occupation-specific rather than job-specific; skills learned can be transferred to another job in the same occupation. Occupations are assigned one of the following six training categories:

Internship/residency. An internship or residency is training that involves preparation in a field such as medicine or teaching, generally under supervision in a professional setting, such as a hospital or classroom. This type of training may occur before one is employed. Completion of an internship or residency program is commonly required for state licensure or certification in fields including medicine, counseling, architecture, and teaching. This category does not include internships that are suggested for advancement. Examples of occupations in the internship/residency category include physicians and surgeons and marriage and family therapists.

Apprenticeship. An apprenticeship is a formal relationship between a worker and sponsor that consists of a combination of on-the-job training and related occupation-specific technical instruction in which the worker learns the practical and theoretical aspects of an occupation. Apprenticeship programs are sponsored by individual employers, joint employer-and-labor groups, and employer associations. The typical apprenticeship

program provides at least 144 hours of occupation-specific technical instruction and 2,000 hours of on-the-job training per year over a 3-to-5 year period. Examples of occupations in the apprenticeship category include electricians and structural iron and steel workers.

Long-term on-the-job training. More than 12 months of on-the-job training or, alternatively, combined work experience and formal classroom instruction are needed for workers to develop the skills to attain competency. Training is occupation specific rather than job specific; therefore, skills learned can be transferred to another job in the same occupation. This on-the-job training category also includes employer-sponsored training programs. Such programs include those offered by fire and police academies and schools for air traffic controllers and flight attendants. In other occupations—nuclear power reactor operators, for example—trainees take formal courses, often provided at the jobsite, to prepare for the required licensing exams. This category excludes apprenticeships. Examples of occupations in the long-term on-the-job training category include opticians and automotive service technicians and mechanics.

Moderate-term on-the-job training. Skills needed for a worker to attain competency in an occupation can be acquired during 1 to 12 months of combined on-the-job experience and informal training. Training is occupation specific rather than job specific; therefore, skills learned can be transferred to another job in the same occupation. This on-the-job training category also includes employer-sponsored training programs. Examples of occupations in the moderate-term category include school bus drivers and advertising sales agents.

Short-term on-the-job training. Skills needed for a worker to attain competency in an occupation can be acquired during 1 month or less of on-the-job experience and informal training. Training is occupation specific rather than job specific; therefore, skills learned can be transferred to another job in the same occupation. This on-the-job training category also includes employer-sponsored training programs. Examples of occupations in the short-term category include retail salespersons and maids and housekeeping cleaners.

None. There is no additional occupation-specific training or preparation typically required to attain competency in the occupation. Examples of occupations that do not require occupation-specific on-the-job training include geographers and pharmacists.

Table 6. Employment and total job openings, by education category, 2010 and projected 2020

(Numbers in thousands)

Typical education needed for entry	Employment				Projected change, 2010–2020		Job openings due to growth and replacement needs, 2010–2020[1]		Median annual wage, May 2010[2]
	Number		Percent distribution						
	2010	2020	2010	2020	Number	Percent	Number	Percent distribution	
Total, all occupations	143,068.2	163,537.1	100.0	100.0	20,468.9	14.3	54,787.4	100.0	$33,840
Doctoral or professional degree	4,409.7	5,286.3	3.1	3.2	876.6	19.9	1,701.8	3.1	87,500
Master's degree	1,986.0	2,417.2	1.4	1.5	431.2	21.7	903.9	1.6	60,240
Bachelor's degree	22,171.1	25,827.2	15.5	15.8	3,656.1	16.5	8,562.4	15.6	63,430
Associate's degree	7,994.6	9,434.6	5.6	5.8	1,440.0	18.0	2,941.0	5.4	61,590
Postsecondary nondegree award	6,524.0	7,624.9	4.6	4.7	1,100.9	16.9	2,389.6	4.4	34,220
Some college, no degree	811.6	953.8	.6	.6	142.2	17.5	362.0	.7	44,350
High school diploma or equivalent	62,089.6	69,665.7	43.4	42.6	7,576.1	12.2	21,745.9	39.7	34,180
Less than high school	37,081.7	42,327.4	25.9	25.9	5,245.7	14.1	16,180.8	29.5	20,070

[1] Total job openings may not equal the sum of replacement needs and employment change. If employment change for a detailed occupation is negative, job openings due to growth are zero and total job openings equal replacement needs.

[2] For wage and salary workers, from the Occupational Employment Statistics survey.

SOURCE: U.S. Bureau of Labor Statistics.

Chart 6. Size and projected 2010–2020 growth of occupations that typically require a high school diploma or equivalent for entry, grouped by typical on-the-job training

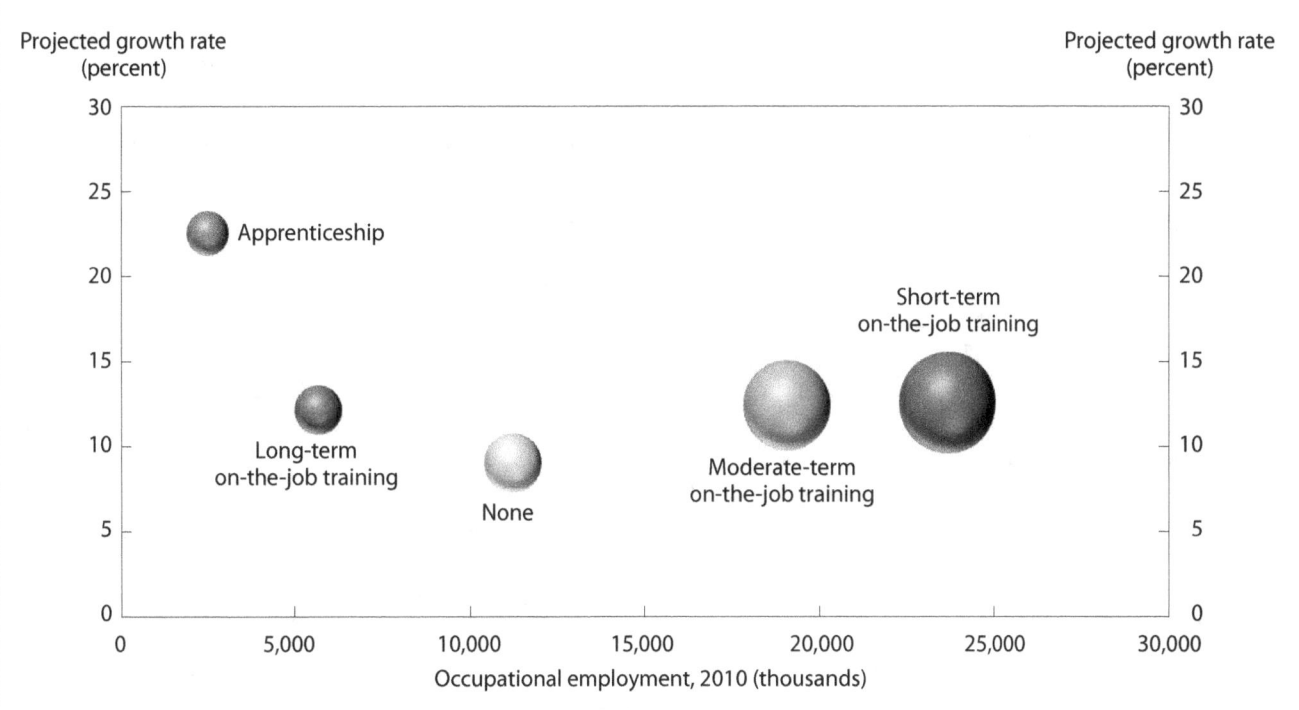

NOTE: Bubble size shows projected growth in the number of jobs.
SOURCE: U.S. Bureau of Labor Statistics.

The new education and training classification system also indicates if work experience in a related occupation is commonly considered necessary by employers for entry or is a commonly accepted substitute for formal types of training. For instance, more than three-quarters of the jobs in occupations that need a bachelor's degree is in occupations that have no related-work-experience requirements. However, bachelor's-degree occupations that do require related work experience, which are often supervisory or management occupations, are generally higher

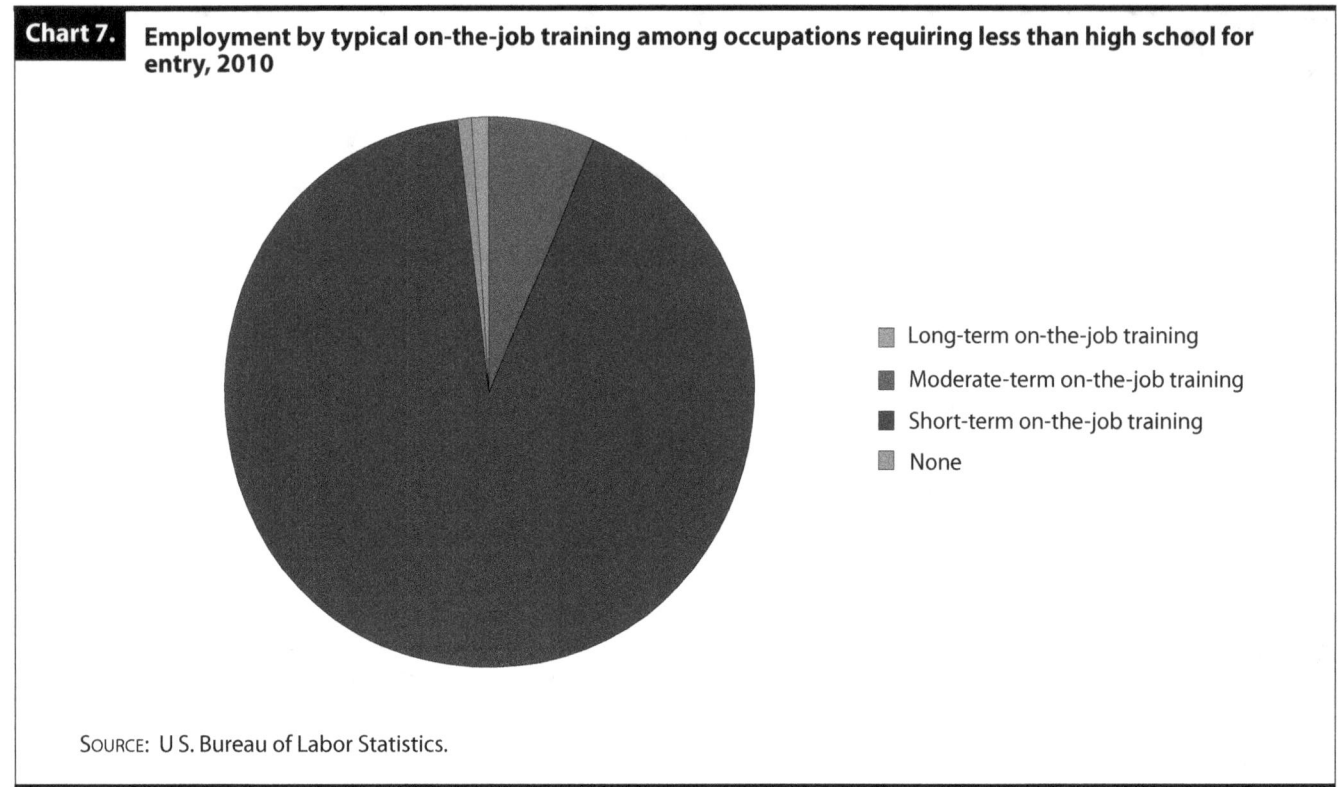

Chart 7. Employment by typical on-the-job training among occupations requiring less than high school for entry, 2010

- Long-term on-the-job training
- Moderate-term on-the-job training
- Short-term on-the-job training
- None

SOURCE: U S. Bureau of Labor Statistics.

paid. The median annual wage for bachelor's-degree occupations with no requirement for work experience in a related occupation was $59,160 in 2010, while the median wage for bachelor's-degree occupations that need 1–5 years of such work experience was $76,090, and in bachelor's-degree occupations that need more than 5 years of such work experience, it was $116,290.

Further employment, projected growth, and earnings data based on the education and training system—including even more detailed groupings which combine education, work experience, and on-the-job training—can be found on the Employment Projections page of the BLS website.[12]

ABOUT 20.5 MILLION JOBS are expected to be added between 2010 and 2020 as the economy continues to recover from the recent recession. The fastest growth is expected in occupations related to healthcare, personal care, and community and social services, fields that remained relatively strong during the recession. However, there

will also be substantial job gains among certain occupations that were severely affected by the recent recession, such as construction occupations and transportation and material moving occupations. Overall, job growth will be faster for occupations that typically need some form of postsecondary education. In addition to jobs arising from growth, 33.7 million job openings will result from the need to replace workers who leave an occupation permanently, creating opportunities in every occupation, even where employment is declining and no new jobs are expected.

Many factors affect the outlook for occupations, including demographic trends, the size of the economy, the types of goods and services that people consume, and technological advancements. The assumptions that BLS used to develop the projections presented here reflect the best information available at the time. New projections are developed and released every 2 years to account for changes in factors such as laws, consumer preferences, and the U.S. economy. □

Notes

[1] The 2012–2013 edition of the *Occupational Outlook Handbook* will be available at **http://www.bls.gov/ooh** in late March 2012.

[2] See Mitra Toossi, "Labor force projections to 2020: a more slowly growing workforce," this issue, pp. 43–64, **http://www.bls.gov/opub/**

mlr/2012/01/art3full.pdf.

[3] People 65 years of age or older spent an average of $4,843 in 2010 on healthcare, compared with $3,157 for all consumers. See 2010 data from the Consumer Expenditures Survey, U.S. Bureau of Labor Statistics, available at **ftp://ftp.bls.gov/pub/special.requests/ce/ standard/2010/age.txt.**

[4] See Kathryn J. Byun and Christopher Frey, "The U.S. economy in 2020, recovery in uncertain times" this issue, pp. 21–42, **http://www. bls.gov/opub/mlr/2012/01/art2full.pdf.**

[5] For more information on the effects of the recession, see Dixie Sommers and James Franklin, "Overview of employment projections to 2020," this issue, pp. 3–20, **http://www.bls.gov/opub/mlr/2012/01/ art1full.pdf.**

[6] See Richard Henderson, "Industry employment and output projections to 2020," this issue, pp. 65–83, **http://www.bls.gov/opub/ mlr/2012/01/art5full.pdf.**

[7] Recessions are identified by the National Bureau of Economic Research (NBER). According to the NBER, the most recent recession began in December 2007 and ended in June 2009. (See **http://www. nber.org/cycles/cyclesmain.html**.) This article uses 2006 data to examine effects of the recession because employment projections are published biennially and no comparable data were released for 2007. Data for 2006 is derived from the data published in Arlene Dohm and Lynn Shniper, "Occupational employment projections to 2016,"

Monthly Labor Review, November 2007, but are adjusted to take into account changes in occupational classifications effective with the 2010 Standard Occupational Classification system.

[8] Wage data used in this article come from the Occupational Employment Statistics (OES) survey, U.S. Bureau of Labor Statistics, **http://www.bls.gov/oes/.**

[9] For a detailed description of the methods used to calculate replacement needs, see the technical documentation accompanying the 2010 to 2020 projections, available at **http://www.bls.gov/emp/ ep_replacements.htm.**

[10] Total job openings may not equal the sum of projected replacement needs and projected employment change. If employment change for a detailed occupation is negative, job openings due to growth are zero and total job openings equal replacement needs. For summary occupations, including the total of all occupations, job openings due to growth are summed from detailed occupations. If some detailed occupations are declining and others are growing, job openings due to growth will not equal the projected employment change.

[11] Table 1.11 on the employment projections page of the BLS website presents data on educational attainment by occupation from the Census Bureau's American Community Survey: **http://www.bls.gov/ emp/ep_table_111.htm.**

[12] In particular, see education and training data at **http://www.bls. gov/emp/ep_education_training_system.htm**